No Room at the Inn: An Advent Call to Justice

The only Advent devotional that weaves together contemplative anti-perfectionism with a fierce, non-negotiable, anti-oppressive call to systemic justice.

by Gregory Simpson

Copyright © 2025 by Gregory Simpson
All rights reserved.
ISBN: 978-1-0694510-1-9

No part of this publication may be reproduced, stored in a retrieval system, or transmitted in any form or by any means—electronic, mechanical, photocopying, recording, or otherwise—without prior written permission of the author, except in the case of brief quotations embodied in critical articles or reviews, or as permitted by Canadian copyright law.

For permission requests, contact:
Gregory Simpson

Email: *pastorgreg18@gmail.com*

This work reflects the author's lived experience, theological exploration, and pastoral voice. While rooted in the Christian tradition, it is written for all who long for meaning, belonging, and sacred space—especially those who have felt displaced by organized religion.

www.gregorysimpson.ca

Dedication

For the ones who are tired of performing.

For the ones who are grieving.

And for all who still believe justice is the only good news worth waiting for.

You are not alone in this.

Table of Contents

December 1..6
   Advent Isn't About Perfection, it's About Longing.........6
December 2..10
   You Don't Have to Pretend You're Okay........................10
December 3..14
   Lament Is Not a Lack of Faith....................................14
December 4..18
   Hope is a Practice...18
December 5..22
   Waiting Is Not Wasted Time.......................................22
December 6..26
   Your Questions Are Welcome Here............................26
December 7..30
   Deconstruction is not a Threat..................................30
December 8..34
   Un-follow the Noise – A Tiny Rule of Life..................34
December 9..38
   Digital Sabbath Is Survival...38
December 10..42
   Gentleness for the Overstimulated.............................42
December 11..46
   Opting Out of Excess: Enough Is Holy.......................46
December 12..49
   Make Room: Hospitality Beyond the Guest List........49
December 13..53
   Small Acts, Big Advent..53
December 14..57
   Climate Grief, Advent Hope......................................57

December 15	60
Ancestors at the Manger	60
December 16	64
Rewriting the Naughty/Nice List	64
December 17	67
You Are Not Too Much, and You Are Not Too Late	67
December 18	70
The Divine Isn't Far Off, It's Right Here	70
December 19	74
Chosen Family at the Manger	74
December 20	78
No Room at the Inn: Housing Is a Sacred Right	78
December 21	82
The Longest Night: Grief and Empty Chairs	82
December 22	86
Justice Is the Gospel	86
December 23	89
A Blessing for Tired Caregivers	89
December 24	92
Joy Is a Form of Resistance	92
December 25	95
Awakening to God's Nearness	95

DECEMBER 1

Advent Isn't About Perfection, it's About Longing.

We begin this Advent journey with an invitation. It is an invitation to step out of the frantic labour of the season and into an honest, holy space.

We know the world will demand performance this season. It will ask for perfectly decorated homes, curated joy, impeccable holiday photos, and effortless family gatherings. In short, it will expect a spirituality of performance.

But the Spirit of Advent offers something else entirely: Advent isn't about perfection and never has been. It's about longing. It is the profound, holy work of waiting, watching, and allowing ourselves to ache for the world as it ought to be.

UNPACKING THE SCRIPTURE

One of the cornerstone texts for this season is not a gentle carol, but a raw, desperate cry from the prophet Isaiah:

> "O that you would tear open the heavens and come down, so that the mountains would quake at your presence " (Isaiah 64:1, NRSVUE)

To understand this cry, we must understand its context. Clearly this is not a prayer of peace and fulfillment. It is the voice of a people who have returned from the trauma of exile, only to find their home, their land, and their hopes in ruins. The promised restoration has not materialized. The systems of oppression are still in place. They are exhausted, disillusioned, and feel profoundly distant from the God who promised deliverance.

This ancient cry lands with familiarity in our own hearts. We, too, find ourselves caught in vast, interlocking systems of injustice that feel far beyond our individual control. We are overrun with awareness of the world's brokenness: some of it impacts us directly, wounding our lives and communities, and some of it floods our senses through news feeds and television screens, leaving us feeling overwhelmed and complicit. Like the people of Isaiah's time we carry a deep and often unarticulated desire for a Divine intervention, a longing for God to simply reach in and fix it.

Their cry, "tear open the heavens," is therefore a recognition of the gap. It is their admission (and ours) of a deep, painful dissonance between our lived reality and God's promise of shalom. They are not pretending to be fine. They are not "trusting the process." They are standing in the rubble of their lives, looking up at what feels like a sealed-off, indifferent sky, and yelling for God to do something.

This is the foundation of Advent: The courageous refusal to accept the status quo; naming the very real pain. Advent does not ask us to ignore the gap between the world as it is and the world we long for. Instead it invites us to see that gap and to speak the truth about it.

THE LIVED REALITY

Over the years, I have learned that the relentless pressure to perform joy at Christmas is not my own. It is a sociological and economic script. Consumer capitalism needs us to feel like we are not enough, because there is profound profit in our exhaustion.

I know the cost of this game. It forces a painful split between the public mask we wear and the lived reality we carry inside.

For many of us, that mask is a conditioned survival mechanism. We learned early—in our families, our workplaces, or our pews—that our authentic, aching self was "too much" or "inconvenient". This is the source of the tyranny of the should that wears us out.

But Advent offers an intervention. It is a quiet, steady hand that invites us to stop, breathe, and tell the truth.

I have had to learn this the hard way: My ache is not a sign that I am failing. My yearning is the raw data of my humanity. My deep desire for justice, for connection, and for rest is not an obstacle to the holy. It is the unquenchable, human evidence that I am a living soul, not a machine of production. It is the holy ground where God is already at work.

Encouragement for Your Day

The invitation for today, then, is one of descent. Instead of striving upward toward an impossible standard of perfection, we are invited downward into the truth of our own present moment.

What if, just for today, you refused to perform? What if you gave yourself permission to simply notice your longing, without judging it or trying to "fix" it?

Take a moment. Breathe. What is the true name of your longing? Are you longing for rest in your exhaustion? Are you longing for justice in a world of inequality? Are you longing for connection in your loneliness?

Honour that. That feeling is not an obstacle to your faith; it *is* your faith. It is the unquenchable evidence that you are made for more than this, and that you know, in your bones, that another version of this world is possible.

A Blessing for Today

Holy One, Divine Mystery, You who are found not in the heights of our performance, but in the depths of our longing. Grant us the courage to lay down the burden of perfection. Grant us the grace to befriend our own ache. Release us from the illusion that we must be whole to be worthy of your presence. Today, and through all the days of this holy, honest season, may our longing not be a burden, but a guide. May it lead us into the quiet, transformative wilderness of Advent, where the real work of hope begins. Amen.

DECEMBER 2

You Don't Have to Pretend You're Okay

We walk today into the heart of an Advent tension. This is the time of year when the culture turns the volume on "jolly" to an almost unbearable level, insisting on a performance of happiness.

But for so many, this season is anything but. It is a time of amplified grief, of profound loneliness, of sitting with the sharp, cold edges of family loss and/or estrangement. It is the season of the empty chair at the table.

If you feel a painful gap between the world's command to be "merry" and the truth of your own heavy heart, I need you to hear this: You don't have to be merry. Just be real. In your pain, you are not failing Advent. You are, perhaps, living its deepest truth.

UNPACKING THE SCRIPTURE

Our faith is not one that bypasses pain; it is one that enters directly into it. We are given one of the most profound, and shortest, verses in all of scripture, from the Gospel of John. Jesus is visiting his friends, Mary and Martha, who are destroyed by the death of their brother, Lazarus. When he sees their raw, devastating sorrow, the text says simply:

> "Jesus wept." (John 11:35)

This is a radical revelation about the nature of the Divine. Jesus does not offer a platitude. He does not tell them to cheer up, to look on the bright side, or to "trust the plan." His most human and most holy response is to honour the reality of their pain by weeping with them.

We follow a God who is, as the prophet Isaiah named, "acquainted with sorrow." The Holy One does not stand aloof from our suffering, demanding we put on a brave face. The Holy One gets in the mess and the tears with us.

This same embodied, messy presence is at the heart of the Christmas story itself. Over the years we have sanitized the nativity, turning it into a pristine, quiet pageant with clean hay and a sleeping baby. But Matthew and Luke write the first Christmas as raw, vulnerable, and dangerous. It is the story of a young, unwed woman in a politically occupied land, a story of displacement, of poverty, and of state-sanctioned threat of violence. There was no safe place to land. It was not "merry"; it was real life in all its precarity.

THE LIVED REALITY

I've had to learn that the cultural command to be "merry" is a form of sociological control. It's the tyranny of toxic positivity, a system that demands our feelings be convenient for others.

I know this from the inside. Psychologically, it forces us into an exhausting, isolating act of emotional labour. I've been in that place of grief where my nervous system is telling a profound, physiological truth, and the world was asking me to perform.

I've learned that to "perform joy" over that grief is to actively disassociate from my own body. It is an act of self-betrayal that creates profound isolation and shame. It's the feeling of being unacceptable at the holiday table.

I've come to know this is a form of spiritual violence. It is a polite faith that shames our sorrow, treating it as an inconvenience or, worse, a theological failure.

But the Advent story is what saves me from this lie. It is not a story that bypasses the flesh. The nativity *is* the story of the flesh; its vulnerability, its pain, its precarity. "Jesus wept" is the ultimate validation. The Divine response to grief is not a platitude, but a shared, embodied sorrow.

This is the truth I hold onto: My sadness is not an obstacle to God; it is the very place the Holy One promises to meet me. My grief does not disqualify me from this season. It places me squarely at the heart of the real Advent story: waiting in the vulnerable, messy, embodied darkness for a light that is genuine, not manufactured.

ENCOURAGEMENT FOR YOUR DAY

The invitation for today is to honour truth, rather than forcing the act of joy.

What if, just for today, you gave yourself permission to not be okay? What if you stopped apologizing for your grief or your loneliness, and instead treated it with a gentle reverence?

Your feelings are not an inconvenience. They are a sign of your love. They are the measure of your heart. Perhaps today, you can light a candle—not in forced celebration, but in quiet solidarity with your own heart, and in memory of what, or who, you have lost.

You are not alone in your sadness. You are, in fact, in holy company, joined with scared Mary and Joseph, and the weeping Christ. You are joined with all who wait honestly in the shadows for the world to be made new.

A Blessing for Today

O Holy Comforter, You who hold our tears and who are well-acquainted with sorrow: Be near today to all who mourn, to all who feel empty, to all who are navigating this season with a heavy heart. Grant us the courage to be real, and save us from the pressure to be "merry." May we find you not in the noise and the glitter, but in the profound, quiet, and holy truth of our own experience. And may we know, in our bones, that we are held and loved. Amen

December 3

Lament Is Not a Lack of Faith

I must be honest about a difficult and necessary truth. I was taught that faith was a synonym for certainty, and that joy meant the absence of sorrow.

My conviction now is that this is a cruel and shallow spirituality. It is a demand for a 'polite' God who reinforces our comfort. But the Advent journey isn't about pretense; it's about reality.

And the reality is that we are living in a world that is aching. I've had to confront that to pretend otherwise is not faith; it is denial.

This is the holy ground of lament. Lament is not a lack of faith. It is, I have come to see, telling the truth in the presence of Love.

UNPACKING THE SCRIPTURE

The biblical tradition, especially in the Psalms, is shockingly, beautifully honest. We have been given an entire prayer book that is, in large part, a book of complaints. This was not an accident. Consider the raw anguish of Psalm 13:

> "How long, O Lord? Will you forget me forever? How long will you hide your face from me? How long must I wrestle with my thoughts and day after day have sorrow in my heart?" (Psalm 13:1-2a)

This is not the prayer of a positive person. This is the prayer of someone in pain who feels utterly abandoned by God. It is an accusation. The compilers of our sacred texts did not edit this out, water it down, or add a polite footnote. They centred it.

They knew that a faith that cannot hold rage, despair, and doubt is a faith that cannot hold a real, suffering human being. The Psalms give us permission and they even give us the language to bring our full, unedited, and often negative selves directly into the presence of the Holy. Lament is the tradition's own antidote to a superficial, transactional spirituality. It is the language of a real relationship, not a script of forced obedience.

THE LIVED REALITY

I know the wound of toxic positivity: that practice of slapping a spiritual platitude on a gaping wound. I've come to see this as a form of spiritual violence, and as a sociological tool of control designed to keep the comfortable comfortable. It demands our silence because our honest, messy, and angry emotions are a threat to the status quo.

I know from the inside what this does: psychologically, it forces a devastating split. We learn that our authentic pain isn't welcome. I've had to unlearn the lie that this repression is holy; it is, in fact, a known trauma response.

What saves me from this is the practice of lament. It is the healthy, necessary, and neurologically-grounded process of telling the truth. It is the act of integration, allowing our bodies and minds to process pain without shame.

This is why lament is a profound act of social healing. A society, like a person, cannot heal from wounds it refuses to name. A faith that demands we pretend keeps us trapped. Lament is the defiant, public, and political act of naming the truth. It is the soul's protest, yes, but it is also the community's first step toward truth and reconciliation.

ENCOURAGEMENT FOR YOUR DAY

The invitation for today is to reclaim this holy, liberating practice. Lament is not an attack on God; it is a profound appeal to God. It is the stubborn, faithful refusal to let God go, even when we are furious. It is the ultimate act of trust, believing that the Divine relationship is real enough and strong enough to hold the full, unedited truth of our experience.

What is the honest, unvarnished cry of your heart today? What injustice in the world makes you rage? What personal sorrow feels unbearable?

Give yourself permission to name it. You don't have to find a silver lining. You don't have to wrap it up with a polite "but I trust you anyway" at the end. Your cry itself is the trust. Telling the truth about your pain, yelling it into the void, is the act of faith. You are staying in the conversation, staying in the relationship, even when it's hard. That is the very definition of a mature, living faith.

A Blessing for Today

O Great Listener, Holy Truth, You who do not fear our darkness, You who wept in the face of grief, You who inspired the Psalmists to yell in your very presence: Save us from cheap grace, easy answers, and polite faith. Give us the holy courage to be real, and the defiant faith to trust you with our rage. This Advent, may our truth-telling be our prayer. May our honesty be the vessel that holds the light. And may we find God not just in our pretense, but in the very heart of our protest. Amen.

December 4

Hope is a Practice

When I look at the world as it is: its injustices, its suffering, its entrenched systems of power, I'll be honest: I am tempted toward despair. In the face of such overwhelming reality, optimism—the passive belief that things will just get better on their own—feels like a luxury at best, or a naive denial at worst.

The Advent journey does not offer us cheap optimism. It offers us something far more resilient, something that must be built, practiced, and embodied.

It offers us hope.

Hope is not a feeling that washes over us; it is a discipline we choose. It is not a passive waiting; it is an active posture. In the words of the great Václav Havel, hope is "an orientation of the spirit." It is the stubborn resistance to despair.

Unpacking the Scripture

The central figure of Advent, Mary, is our great teacher in the practice of hope. When the Divine invitation comes to her, she is a young, poor, unwed woman in a colonized, occupied territory. She has zero social, political, or economic power. She has every reason for cynicism, every reason to protect herself, every reason to say "no" to this dangerous, world-altering call.

Her "yes" is not passive submission. It is a radical, courageous act of alignment with God's dream for the world. And her song, the Magnificat, is the anthem of this defiant practice. She sings:

> "[God] has brought down the powerful from their thrones, and lifted up the lowly; [God] has filled the hungry with good things, and sent the rich away empty." (Luke 1:52-53)

We must understand what is happening here. Mary is not singing about a past event. As she sings, the powerful are still firmly on their thrones. The lowly are still oppressed. She and her people are still hungry.

This is a profound, prophetic act of hope. She is standing in the midst of a broken reality and announcing the new reality of God's justice as if it is already coming true. She is practicing the future into being. This is hope as a verb, an act of co-creation with the Divine.

The Lived Reality

Optimism is fragile. My real struggle is with despair and cynicism. These are not just bad moods; they are profound sociological and psychological states. I now understand that despair is the *goal* of oppressive systems—an overwhelmed, fragmented, and hopeless populace is a compliant one.

Cynicism, meanwhile, is often a protective, isolating trauma response. It is the part of our psyche that, having seen the rubble (Day 1) and named the ache (Day 3), decides to check out to avoid further wounding. It is a profound failure of imagination, a collapse of the spirit into individualism.

What saves me from this is Advent hope. This is the disciplined, neurological practice of resisting this collapse. It is not the opposite of lament; it is the partner of lament. It is the choice to walk alongside our holy, honest ache without being consumed by it.

Encouragement for Your Day

The invitation for today is one of endurance. If you are burnt out, if you are tired of the fight, if you have been an activist, a caregiver, a teacher, or just a compassionate human long enough to be weary... you do not have to feel hopeful.

Your only invitation is to practice hope.

And this practice can be small. It can be as quiet as getting out of bed when despair tells you to stay down. It can be writing the letter, making the call, checking on your neighbour, or donating the five dollars. It can be the act of resting, which is itself an act of resistance against a system that demands constant, frantic production.

You are not asked to save the world. You are simply invited to participate, with your small, stubborn "yes," in the great, world-changing "Yes" of Mary. That is how the incarnation continues.

A Blessing for Today

O Holy One, Author of all just dreams and Ground of all being, Save us from the illusion of cheap optimism. When our spirits are tired and our hearts are heavy with the world's pain, grant us not a fleeting feeling, but a stubborn resolve. Root us in the deep, quiet practice of hope. Make us resilient. Make us brave. Make us, like Mary, people who dare to say 'yes' to your impossible dream of justice, and then live each day as if it is already coming true. Amen.

December 5

Waiting Is Not Wasted Time

We live in a culture obsessed with doing. Our worth is too often measured by our productivity, our forward movement, our visible achievements.

I'll be honest: I am not good at waiting. I was conditioned to believe my worth is in what I do. To be stuck—in a job hunt, in grief, or in healing—is treated as a failure of will. That feeling of "stuckness" is a space I have learned to fear; it feels like a void, an emptiness, a waste.

But the Advent journey reframes this entirely. It asks us to consider that this liminal space is not empty at all. It is, in fact, the most potent space we can occupy. Advent says waiting isn't wasting. It's where new life forms.

UNPACKING THE SCRIPTURE

The entire hinge of the incarnation story rests on two women *waiting*. We have Elizabeth, who has waited a lifetime, past all cultural "productivity," for a child. And we have Mary, thrown into a sudden, terrifying, and vulnerable wait. Their story is not one of public action, but of hidden, holy gestation.

My understanding of this was transformed when I encountered the deep well of womanist theology. This wisdom, born from the experience and endurance of Black women, taught me to honour what the dominant, hurried, and disembodied culture discards. It reclaims the wisdom of the body, the sacredness of the dark, and the holiness of *process*. It knows what it means to birth new life in impossible circumstances.

When Mary, in her own new pregnancy, greets Elizabeth, the baby in Elizabeth's womb *leaps* (Luke 1:41). The very first recognition of the incarnation happens here—not in a temple or a palace, but in the hidden, embodied, *waiting* space shared between two women. God's most profound, world-changing work is almost always done in the dark, in the quiet, in the womb, far from the frantic pace of the world.

THE LIVED REALITY

I have had to learn, slowly and painfully, to unlearn the lie of hustle culture, that sociological system obsessed with measurable productivity. It is the system that taught me my worth is synonymous with my visible achievements.

Psychologically, this created a terror of the in-between time; the waiting, the healing, the not-knowing. When I am in that space, my conditioned mind craves control and validation, interpreting the "stuckness" as a personal failure. It is a disembodied state that disconnects me from my own body and its rhythms.

My healing from this has been guided by the deep wisdom of womanist theology. This lens, born from the endurance of Black women, calls me to honour what our hurried, disembodied culture discards: the sacredness of the body, the dark, and the gestational process.

This is a biological and neurological truth I've had to reclaim: Gestation is not wasting time. It is the most complex, demanding, and creative work imaginable. The same is true for our minds and spirits. The dark and stuck periods are not an absence of life; they are the fertile, quiet, neurological conditions necessary for new pathways and new resilience to be formed.

This is the new truth I tell myself: I am not "stuck." I am in a sacred, formative process.

ENCOURAGEMENT FOR YOUR DAY

The invitation for today is to reframe your "stuckness." It is not a problem to be solved; it is a space to be inhabited.

What if, just for today, you stopped fighting the wait? What if you stopped calling it "wasting time" and began to call it "gestation"?

Be present to the darkness. Be gentle with the not-knowing. Trust the hidden, slow, cellular work that is happening within you. You are not being left behind. You are being *formed*. This is the deep, counter-cultural wisdom of Advent.

A Blessing for Today

O Holy One, Creator of all new life, You who chose the dark of the womb to begin our salvation: Quiet the anxious voices that tell us we are unproductive or left behind. Help us to honour this holy, hidden time of waiting. Grant us the patience of Elizabeth and the quiet courage of Mary. May we trust the sacred, formative work you are doing in the dark, believing that new life is taking root, right now, within us. Amen.

DECEMBER 6

Your Questions Are Welcome Here

I must speak today about one of the great wounds of religious life: the fear of questions. Many of us were raised in a culture of certainty, where faith was presented as a set of non-negotiable answers. To question was to betray. To doubt was to be on a "slippery slope" to apostasy.

But this is a profound and damaging misunderstanding of faith. This is the ego's demand for a manageable, controllable God. **A faith that cannot survive a question is not faith—it is fear.** It is a security system for the false self, not a resting place for the soul.

UNPACKING THE SCRIPTURE

We have done a great disservice to the disciple Thomas, branding him "the Doubter." In truth, Thomas is perhaps one of the most courageous of the group. He is the one who refuses to settle for a second-hand, reported faith. He is the one who holds out for a real, embodied encounter. He must know for himself.

And when Jesus finally appears to him, he does not shame Thomas. He does not banish him or quote scripture at him. He invites the question. He offers his very wounds as the text to be read:

> "Put your finger here. See my hands. Reach out your hand and put it in my side. Stop doubting and believe." (John 20:27, NRSV paraphrased)

This is a radical revelation. The resurrected Christ does not meet Thomas with a show of invulnerable, triumphalist power, but with an invitation into shared vulnerability. The wound becomes the place of knowing. The doubt becomes the doorway to the deepest encounter.

THE LIVED REALITY

Here is the hard truth I've had to confront: "certainty" is a sociological tool of control. The culture of certainty you were raised in was not an accident; it was a system designed to maintain institutional power. The "slippery slope" isn't a theological argument; I now understand it's a psychological threat used to enforce conformity.

Psychologically, this system conditions us to fear ambiguity. It fosters a brittle cognitive rigidity, a state where our identity is so fused with a set of answers that any question feels like a personal attack. Neurologically, this is the brain's threat-response systems in overdrive. An honest doubt, which should be processed as new data, is instead perceived by the amygdala as an existential danger.

I've come to see deconstruction as the agonizing process of that system breaking down. It is the brain's higher-order functions finally wrestling with the reality of the world's wounds and injustice, which the old system's answers can no longer explain away.

Doubt is not the opposite of faith. Doubt is the healthy, adaptive, neurological function of a soul refusing to settle for a second-hand, received faith. Like Thomas, it is the sacred, embodied insistence on a real encounter.

Encouragement for Your Day

The invitation for today is to befriend your questions. If you are in a season of doubt, you are not failing. You are not lost. You are in a holy, liminal space.

Do not rush for new, easy answers to replace the old ones. That is just rebuilding the same house of cards with different materials. The invitation of Advent is to wait in the unknown, to sit with the mystery.

What if, just for today, you honoured your curiosity as a sacred impulse? What if you saw your doubt not as a sin, but as a sign that you are no longer willing to settle for a second-hand, pre-packaged God? You are being invited out of the house of cards and onto the solid, open, and wondrous ground of relationship.

A Blessing for Today

O Holy Mystery, you who are the Source of all knowing, yet are beyond all our answers: Bless our doubts. Bless our questions. Bless the holy, burning "why" that rises in our hearts. Save us from the fear that masquerades as faith, and from the certainty that blinds us to your presence. Grant us the courage of Thomas, to seek an honest encounter. This Advent, may your questions be a lantern in the dark, leading you not to a fragile answer, but deeper into the vast, living, and welcoming heart of God. Amen.

DECEMBER 7

Deconstruction is not a Threat

There is a word that causes great fear in our communities: deconstruction. For those experiencing it, it feels like a terrifying freefall, a loss of identity. For those watching a loved one go through it, it looks like rebellion or a tragic loss of faith. We are conditioned to see it as a threat.

But what if this painful unraveling is not the *end* of faith, but a necessary, holy, and ancient part of its maturation? **Jesus didn't build walls—he cracked them open. Deconstruction can be a sacred path.**

UNPACKING THE SCRIPTURE

We must be clear: Jesus was a master deconstructor. He was a profound threat to the religious systems of his day not because he was an outsider, but because he was an insider who knew the texts and traditions so well, he could expose where the system had betrayed the God it claimed to serve.

When the Pharisees, the guardians of the system, confronted him about his disciples breaking the 'tradition of the elders' (in this case, rules about ritual hand-washing), they were defending their 'container.' Jesus, in his response, breaks the container open to reveal the content:

> "Why do your disciples break the tradition of the elders?... [Jesus] answered them, 'And why do you break the commandment of God for the sake of your tradition?... This people honors me with their lips, but their hearts are far from me; in vain do they worship me, teaching human precepts as doctrines.'" (Matthew 15:2-3, 8-9 NRSV)

With this response, Jesus deconstructs their system of control. He reveals that their traditions and their religious rules had become idols, and that they were sacrificing the very commandment of God on the altar of religious certainty. He did this constantly—with purity laws, with temple-based power, with social hierarchies. He was always cracking open the hard, brittle shell of religion to find the living heart of Love.

THE LIVED REALITY

I've come to see that the faith many of us are handed — the one we inherit or absorb without question — isn't neutral. It's built. Shaped by institutions, by social forces, by the need to preserve order and control. It gives us language and structure, but it also functions like a container: a set of boundaries for what's acceptable to feel, to ask, to believe. And that structure tends to work… until it doesn't.

For me, the breaking began when real life, things like grief, injustice, and unanswerable questions, started pressing against the container. The system didn't have space for that kind of raw, unresolvable pain. It tried to give answers instead of presence. It had certainty, but somehow not truth. And when the structure finally cracked, it wasn't a clean break. It felt like something in me was dying.

And that makes sense. Because neurologically, something is dying. When we start to question or dismantle the faith structures that once held us, the old pathways — the ones shaped by certainty, simplicity, and fear — begin to break apart. And for a while, it's just disorientation. Like freefall. Like tomb-space. The brain doesn't know where to land, and neither does the heart.

But here's what I've learned, both in my own unravelling and in walking with others through theirs: that collapse isn't the end of faith. It's the beginning of something more honest. More human. More alive. It's not a loss of God; it's a refusal to keep forcing God into a container too small to hold reality. It's not destruction for the sake of destruction. It's the holy, painful work of clearing out what never belonged in the first place.

What grows in its place is slower. Less shiny. But it can breathe. It can hold tension. It can hold you. And that's worth everything.

ENCOURAGEMENT FOR YOUR DAY

If feel like you are in that messy middle, hear this: You are not lost. You are on holy ground.

This path is not a sign of your failure; it is a sign of your spiritual courage. You are refusing to settle for a small, brittle, tribal god. You are refusing to worship the container.

The invitation for today is to be incredibly gentle with yourself. You are in the wilderness. You are in the tomb. This is the Advent work of waiting in the dark. Trust yourself in the midst of the process. You are not "falling away" or "backsliding." You are being invited deeper into the vast, mysterious, and living heart of Love.

A Blessing for Today

O Holy One, Divine Architect, You who are our foundation, and You who are the loving force that cracks open all that is false: Be with the ones who are sitting in the dust of their own certainty. Bless their courage. Soothe their fear. Remind them that this falling apart is a holy prelude to being put back together in a new, more honest way. And for those of us watching from the outside, grant us the grace of compassion over judgment, that we might be companions, not accusers, as we all journey deeper into the mystery of your Love. Amen.

DECEMBER 8

Un-follow the Noise – A Tiny Rule of Life

We are living in a state of profound fragmentation, not by accident, but by design. I have come to realize that my attention is the most valuable thing I own, and it is under constant assault. An entire "attention economy" is engineered to harvest our consciousness. This constant stimulation fractures our spirit, keeping us in a reactive, shallow, and anxious state. We are not just experiencing the noise; we are being conditioned by it.

Advent is a season of profound resistance. But I know I cannot make room for the Holy if every corner of my inner life is already filled. The invitation for today is not another grand, exhausting project of self-improvement. Instead, it is a set of small, "fleshy" anchors to ground us in what is real.

UNPACKING THE SCRIPTURE

I want us to listen to the prophet Elijah who provides a powerful model for this work. In 1 Kings 19, Elijah is the epitome of the burnt-out, disillusioned prophet. He is running for his life, hiding in a cave, and in a deep, dark night of the soul, waiting for a Divine encounter.

He expects God to show up in the spectacle: the wind, the earthquake, the fire. Isn't this exactly how our ego, and the systems of Empire, expect power to work: with noise, drama, and overwhelming force? But the text is clear: God is not in the noise.

> "...and after the fire, a sound of sheer silence." (1 Kings 19:12b)

The Hebrew for "a sound of sheer silence" could also be translated as "a thin, quiet sound." God's power is of an entirely different order. It whispers. And to hear it, I've had to learn that I must first cultivate my own inner silence.

THE LIVED REALITY

I have had to learn this the hard way: that noise isn't neutral. It is a sociological system engineered to keep me in a neurological state of high alert, a reactive fight or flight mode.

I know the cost of this. This constant, low-grade agitation is the enemy of presence. It makes me disembodied, living in my head, and fractures my capacity for the deep thought and empathy that are the hallmarks of a living soul.

This is not a spiritual problem I can just believe away. It is a physical and mental health problem that requires practice that gest us back into our bodies. This "tiny rule of life" is that practice.

"A Deep Breath" is not a life hack; it is a neurological intervention. It is the fastest, most effective way I have found to communicate to my own nervous system that I am safe, down-regulating it from fight or flight and allowing me to be present in my own body. "Ten Minutes Offline" is my act of reclaiming my "sacred attention" from the sociological machine designed to steal it.

Encouragement for Your Day

The invitation for today is a "tiny rule of life" composed of three anchors:

- **A Deep Breath.** This is an intentional physical act. It is the simple, profound practice of remembering I have a body that needs breath and anchoring my scattered spirit back into the present moment: the only place God is.

- **A Small Kindness.** The noise makes us obsessed with our own agenda: "What do I need, what am I missing?" A small, intentional act of kindness (sending a congratulatory or grateful text, letting a car in ahead of us) breaks that narcissistic spell. It is a micro-practice of love, connecting us to the "other" and reminding us we are part of an interconnected whole.

- **Ten Minutes Offline.** Your attention is one of the most sacred things you possess. To deliberately go offline for just ten minutes is a radical act. You are not producing. You are not consuming. You are just being. You are reclaiming your sacred attention, creating a tiny, silent clearing where the Holy can be born.

A breath. A kindness. Ten minutes. This is how we begin to unfollow the noise and practice resurrection.

A Blessing for Today

O Holy One, you who are the Sound of Sheer Silence: Our world is so loud, and our souls are so tired. Grant us the courage to unplug from the noise that fractures. Grant us the simple grace to be kind. Grant us the profound, life-giving gift of our own breath. This Advent, in the midst of the frantic and the fractured, may we have the wisdom to seek the tiny, quiet spaces where you are already waiting. Amen.

December 9
Digital Sabbath Is Survival

We are living within a machine that is precision-engineered to harvest our consciousness. This is not hyperbole; it is the business model of the age. The algorithms that govern our online lives are not neutral. They are designed to commodify our anxiety. They profit from our rage-bait, our envy, and our doom-scrolling.

This system is a false god that demands our constant, anxious attention. It is a "principality and power" that thrives on our exhaustion and profits from our fragmentation.

In the face of such a system, the practice of Sabbath (specifically, a Digital Sabbath) is not a quaint, optional self-care luxury. It is an act of spiritual and political resistance. It is a necessary practice for the survival of the soul.

UNPACKING THE SCRIPTURE

When Jesus was confronted by the religious authorities for breaking their Sabbath rules, he offered a profound deconstruction of their system:

> "The Sabbath was made for humankind, not humankind for the Sabbath." (Mark 2:27)

The keepers of the law had turned a divine gift of liberation into a heavy, human-made burden of control. They had made people subservient to the system itself, forgetting that the system was only ever meant to serve life and wholeness.

It might be a slight stretch, but I'd like to compare this to a different system we now serve: the 24/7 demand of the algorithm. It is a new legalism, one that insists we must always be on, always available, always consuming, and always performing. To step away, to rest, feels like a transgression. Jesus's words are a radical permission slip for us today: This technology was made for us; we were not made for it. We are called to be masters of our tools, not servants to them.

THE LIVED REALITY

I've had to learn that the "new legalism" Jesus confronted isn't just the 9-to-5 grindstone. It's the 24/7 sociological demand for a curated life.

I know what this feels like, and I see it in the people I walk with. It's the carefully curated versions of friends, influencers, and strangers that create an impossible, invisible law. A law that dictates we must not only be productive but performatively tidy, happy, and "good enough" for public consumption.

We must learn to see this system for what it is: a machine precision-engineered to generate shame and inadequacy. It is designed to feed the comparison, the envy, and the profound anxiety that our real, messy, human lives are a failure. This is how it commodifies our anxiety by making us feel not good enough and then selling us the solution.

A digital Sabbath, for me, is therefore not a luxury. It has become a non-negotiable mental health practice. It is my political act of unplugging from the shame-machine. It is how I, in my own life, side with Jesus's declaration that my real, messy, un-postable life was not made to be a servant to this system.

Encouragement for Your Day

The invitation for today is a small, subversive act of prayer. It is an incarnational prayer—one that brings you back into your body and into the real, physical world.

Your attention is the vessel of your love. Where you choose to place it is what you worship.

So, as an act of holy resistance, what if you simply... unplugged? Not as a punishment, but as a liberation.

Close three apps. Open a window. Take a deep breath.

Feel the air. Listen to the sounds of your *actual* room. That is prayer, too. It is the radical act of choosing the *real* over the *virtual*. It is "coming home" to your body and to the immediate, tangible presence of God, which can only ever be found in the *here and now*.

A Blessing for Today

O Holy One, Ground of all Being, You who are found in the real: Free us from the machines that harvest our anxiety. Grant us the holy courage to unplug, to rest, and to resist. May we have the wisdom to reclaim our sacred attention, and the grace to find you, not in the endless scroll of the virtual, but in the real air, the real light, and the real, quiet presence of our own holy lives. Amen.

December 10

Gentleness for the Overstimulated

The culture's version of this season is, for many, a sensory assault. It is a demand for performance that is not just spiritual but physical. The lights are too bright and they blink. The music is constant and repetitive. The crowds are chaotic. The pressure to be "on," to socialize, and to perform joy is immense.

For the introvert, the highly sensitive person, and our neurodivergent friends, this is not festive; it can be a kind of sensory hell. It is an environment that pushes the human nervous system past its limits.

The invitation for today is one of profound gentleness. It is a quiet permission slip. Three slow breaths count as prayer. So does saying, "I need quiet."

Unpacking the Scripture

This state of overwhelm is not a modern failure; it is a profoundly human experience, one named in the Gospels themselves. In Mark 6, Jesus and his disciples are at their limit. They are so inundated by the demands of the crowds, the needs, and the constant motion that they are utterly burnt out. The text is strikingly practical:

> "And he said to them, 'Come away by yourselves to a quiet place, and rest a while.' For many were coming and going, and they had no leisure even to eat." (Mark 6:31)

"Many were coming and going" is perhaps the most accurate description of the frantic energy of December. And Jesus's response is not a pep talk. It is not a call to "power through" or "try harder." It is a pastoral intervention. It is a radical, practical command to retreat, to separate, and to rest. He names the "quiet place" as the necessary antidote to the chaos. This is not an escape *from* holy work; it *is* the holy work.

THE LIVED REALITY

I know the feeling of the sensory assault this season demands. The blinking lights, the constant music, the chaotic crowds. That this isn't just festive; it's a sociological demand for a specific kind of sensory performance.

Neurologically, sensory overload is more than just triggering a bad attitude; it is a physiological state. My heart our neurodivergent siblings, whose brains process sensory input differently, this environment can be a sensory hell. But this is no longer a niche experience. We are all part of an epidemic of overstimulation, with our nervous systems constantly pushed past their capacity and into a state of fight, flight, or freeze.

I also know the shame that follows, the system then shames our lived reality. When our body is telling us "I am overwhelmed," the culture calls us a Scrooge, antisocial, or difficult. This forces a painful split—we betray ourselves by performing to avoid the shame, which only leads to deeper burnout.

Your limits, therefore, are not a spiritual failure. Here is the truth I hold onto: they are neurological messengers. Your body, in its overwhelm, is telling the truth. Honouring your need for quiet is not an anti-Advent act. It is a holy, human act, obeying the Christ-like invitation to come away when the "coming and going" is too much.

Encouragement for Your Day

The invitation for today is to give yourself radical permission. You have permission to leave the party early. You have permission to say "no" to an invitation. You have permission to sit in a dark, quiet room. You have permission to wear your headphones while shopping.

You are not "ruining the fun." You are protecting your peace. You are practicing an accessible faith. You are honouring the way you were made.

The real Advent is quiet. It is dark. It is internal. It is gestation. It is the opposite of the culture's loud, frantic demands. Your need for quiet is not a distraction from Advent; it is an invitation into its true, gentle heart.

A Blessing for Today

O Holy One, you who invite us to the quiet place: Save us from the tyranny of the noise, and from the shame of feeling "too sensitive." Grant us the profound courage to honour our limits, to heed our body's truth, and to accept your holy invitation to rest. Help us to find you, not in the chaos of the "coming and going," but in the gentle, healing, sacred quiet you have promised for our souls. Amen.

DECEMBER 11

Opting Out of Excess: Enough Is Holy

We are living in the high holy days of the god of More. This season, more than any other, is an assault of manufactured lack. The core message of consumerism is not, "Here is something beautiful," but rather, "You are not enough without this." It is a frantic, anxious, and exhausting message. It creates a deep spiritual dis-ease, a sense of guilt, and a panic that our love can only be measured by our spending.

But the Advent journey is a path of profound resistance to this idol. It is a quiet, steady turn from the spirituality of *excess* to the spirituality of sufficiency. What if the holiest, most rebellious, and most liberating word we could practice this season is **enough**?

UNPACKING THE SCRIPTURE

The logic of consumerism is rooted in fear—the fear of not having enough, of *being* not enough. The author of the Letter to the Hebrews offers a direct antidote. It is a call to shift our entire foundation of security:

> "Keep your lives free from the love of money, and be content with what you have; for [God] has said, 'I will never leave you or forsake you.'" (Hebrews 13:5)

This is not a purity law about money itself. It is a profound invitation to stop loving *what money represents*: a false sense of security, control, and worth. The text commands us to be "content," not because our material situation is perfect, but because our *source* is different. The foundation is not our bank account; it is the unbreakable *presence* of the Divine. The promise is not *stuff*; the promise is *God*.

This reorients everything. It moves us from a life of anxious accumulation to one of grounded presence.

THE LIVED REALITY

We are surrounded by a sociological system of manufactured lack. Consumer capitalism, the god of More, is an economic model and also a spiritual one. Its core message is "You are not enough," a constant, psychological assault on our human sense of worth.

Psychologically, this system conditions us to live in a state of comparison. It creates a bottomless pit of anxious striving, where our worth is only ever measured in relation to others: "Do I have enough?" "Am I enough?" This is the source of the profound dis-ease and anxious accumulation that define the season.

The Advent story offers a profound, human intervention. It confronts the lie of scarcity with the truth of sufficiency. The manger is the ultimate counter-protest: the world-tilting mystery is not one of excess, but of radical presence. Your human soul does not need to acquire worth; you are already enough.

Encouragement for Your Day

The invitation for today is to practice the holy, rebellious act of saying "enough."

You are *enough*. Your love is *enough*. What you have is *enough*.

This is not a call to inaction, but a call to redefine blessing. We have been sold a cheap, empire-based definition of blessing that means material wealth. The Gospel reclaims blessing as sufficiency (having what you truly need for today), community (the messy, real presence of others), and care (the flow of love between us).

The most precious, sacred gift you have to offer this season is not your credit card. It is your quiet, undivided, unhurried presence. That is the only gift that can satisfy the real, holy hunger of the human heart.

A Blessing for Today

O Holy One, You who are our Sufficiency, Our true source and our true home: Save us from the tyranny of 'more.' Quiet the frantic, screaming voice of consumerism that tells us we are not enough. Release us from the lie that our worth is in what we buy. In this season of noise, help us find the sacred, liberating, and peaceful whisper of 'enough.' May we rest in your presence, and may our own presence be our most precious gift. Amen.

DECEMBER 12

Make Room: Hospitality Beyond the Guest List

This is the high season of hospitality. It is a word I have often used for guest lists, table settings, and centrepieces. I've had to confront that this was my hospitality of performance, aesthetics, and, ultimately, control. It was a hospitality that made me feel good because it reinforced the walls of "us" and "them".

But the Gospel demands a far more costly and radical practice. It demands a hospitality of justice. Hospitality has nothing to do with table settings; it's all about making sure everyone can get through the door. Advent is the great audit of our inns, and it asks one, piercing question: Who is still left outside?

UNPACKING THE SCRIPTURE

The entire, world-tilting mystery of the Incarnation pivots on a single, devastating line of text. It is a story of a profound failure of hospitality:

> "...because there was no room for them in the inn."
> (Luke 2:7b)

We have sentimentalized this line, imagining a flustered but kind innkeeper. I've come to see the text as colder and more systemic. It is a statement of systemic exclusion. The *kataluma* (the "inn" or "guest room") was not available to them.

Why? My pastoral reading is that they were the wrong people. They were poor. They were under the suspicion of scandal. They were subjects of Empire, in town for a census—a tool of political and economic control. The "inn," as I now understand it represented the entire interlocking system of commerce, social purity, and power. And that system had no space for them. God's arrival, therefore, did not happen in the centre of welcome, power, and acceptance; it happened in the messy, cold, excluded margins that power itself had created.

THE LIVED REALITY

I've come to see that my hospitality of the guest list was a primary function of my own sociological identity-making. I was living in a culture that taught me to build my sense of self by defining who is "Us" and who is "Them".

I now understand this as a deeply human, psychological drive for safety and control. My "inn," therefore, was not just my physical space; it was my carefully protected boundary. My "centrepiece hospitality" was the act of reinforcing that boundary to protect my comfort and maintain control.

I had to be honest that the "others"; people the culture names as "Them", feel like a psychological threat to that control. The unhoused person, the person whose body or identity challenged my norms: I felt, in my gut, that their needs cost me my comfort and my preferences.

The failure in the Advent story is this: the system functioned perfectly. It did what it was designed to do: it protected "Us" by excluding "Them".

Justice hospitality, I am learning, is the terrifying, human work of letting go of my preferences and my control. This work forces me to ask the hard questions: Is there a physical ramp? Is there a quiet room for the neurodivergent? Are queer and trans people truly safe and celebrated here, not just tolerated?

And as a white man, this work demands something more: it demands I ask if I am centring my own voice and culture. Am I intentionally seeking out, listening to, and submitting to the leadership of BIPOC and other racialized voices, or am I just looking for a token at the edge? This is my conscious decision to move from a psychology of control to a spirituality of encounter.

Encouragement for Your Day

The invitation for today is to conduct a holy audit. Look at the "inns" you control—your home, your social media feed, your assumptions, your church, your heart.

Ask the hard, holy question: "Who still has no room here?"

This is not an invitation to guilt. I've found that guilt is often just my old psychological drive for control trying to make the problem about me again. This is an invitation to *awareness*. Advent is the season of making room. That is not a passive, sentimental feeling. It is the active, sacred, and sometimes costly work of looking at a wall and deciding to be the one who grabs the hammer.

A Blessing for Today

O Holy One, You who were turned away at the door, You who are still turned away: Forgive us for the comfort of our "inns" and the beauty of our centrepieces. Save us from a hospitality that costs us nothing and changes no one. This Advent, make us brave. Make us into people who see walls and ask "why?" Make us into a real room for all, that we might not miss your arrival in the face of the stranger we have kept outside. Amen.

DECEMBER 13

Small Acts, Big Advent

We live in an age of overwhelming information. We are made aware of every global injustice, every climate catastrophe, every systemic wound, all at once.

I know the feeling of being utterly paralyzed by the sheer scale of the world's pain. I've learned that when I'm faced with this, my mind often does one of two things: it either leaps toward a grandiose fantasy of saving the world, or it collapses into a cynical despair, a compassion fatigue that tells me: "Nothing I do can possibly matter."

Both are forms of paralysis; a very human, psychological self-defense against the overwhelm.

But the Advent path is not a path of grandiosity or despair. It is the path of human-scale love. It is the practice of defiant, small, embodied hope. Tiny revolutions count—one email, one meal, one moment of care.

Unpacking the Scripture

In Matthew 25, Jesus gives us the great, final audit of a human life. And it is shockingly, radically simple. He does not ask, "Did you construct a perfect theology? Did you solve the eco-political crisis of your day?"

He collapses the entire, massive, abstract concept of "serving God" into the smallest, most immediate, most human-scale acts:

> "I was hungry and you gave me something to eat, I was thirsty and you gave me something to drink, I was a stranger and you invited me in..." (Matthew 25:35)

This is the principle of incarnation. The *Universal* (God, Love, Justice) is not found "out there" in the abstract. It is found *only* in the *Particular* —the hungry neighbour, the thirsty person, the excluded stranger right in front of us. He is saying, "You don't have to fix the *concept* of 'global hunger.' Just... feed *one person*."

The Lived Reality

I know this compassion fatigue intimately. It's a very human, psychological state of paralysis. I've had to learn that my mind, when overwhelmed by the bigness of the world's problems, wants to be the hero. And if I cannot be the hero who fixes everything, my impulse is to do nothing. It is a paralysis of the grandiose, a defense mechanism to protect me from the pain of my own smallness.

What saves me from this trap is not a grand plan. It is the human-scale wisdom of Matthew 25. The part of me that is connected to the world, my shared humanity, is not concerned with being a hero. It is concerned with connection.

This is the lesson of Jesus' mother Mary. Her "yes" was not a global strategic plan. It was a personal, hidden, terrifying "yes" that happened in a quiet room. It was the smallest, most particular, most human "yes" imaginable, and the entire cosmos pivoted on it. The revolution always begins in the small.

An Encouragement for Your Day

The invitation for today is to be liberated from the paralysis of "too big." You are not asked to end all suffering. You are simply invited to participate, with your two hands, in the *one* act of love that is in front of you.

That one email to your local politician. That one meal for your sick neighbour. That one $10 donation. That one hard, honest conversation about justice.

This is not a distraction from the real work. This *is* the real work, made incarnate. Your small, faithful act is not a drop in the ocean; it is the ocean itself, contained in a single, holy drop. It is the revolution, made small enough for your hands to hold today.

A Blessing for Today

O Holy One, You who are found in the particular, You who came to us in the small, the overlooked, and the right-in-front-of-us: Save us from the paralysis of the grandiose. Save us from the despair that convinces us our smallness is a weakness. This Advent, when our hearts are overwhelmed by the world's pain, grant us the holy clarity to see the one cup of water, the one act of care, the one 'yes' that you are asking of us today. And may we trust that in this small, faithful act, the whole revolution of your Love is already present. Amen.

DECEMBER 14
Climate Grief, Advent Hope

It is time to be honest about the grief that is choking us. It is the great, unspoken terror in our pews and at our tables: the eco-anxiety, the climate *dread*.

We see the headlines—the fires, the floods, the vanishing species, the melting ice—and we feel a profound, agonizing sorrow for a world that is being actively destroyed.

Let's be absolutely clear. This is not an "anxiety disorder." This is not a "lack of faith." **Your grief is a sane, moral, and holy response to the truth.** It is right to mourn the world we are losing. The time for spiritualizing this away, or for "polite" prayers, is long over. Our house is on fire, and we are being called to sound the alarm.

UNPACKING THE SCRIPTURE

I have had to confess that for centuries, the global church has been criminally complicit. It has taught a toxic, dualistic theology that tells us this physical world is disposable: a waiting room for a spiritual heaven.

I have come to see this for what it is: a heresy that gave Christian-formed cultures the spiritual permission to plunder and destroy creation for profit.

The central, shattering claim of Advent is what saves me from this lie. It is the "in-the-flesh" truth of the story

> "The Word became flesh." (John 1:14)

I've had to learn that the Greek word used here, sarx, doesn't just mean a human body. It means matter. It is soil, water, breath, muscle, and nerve. It is the entire ecosystem.

This is the truth that radicalized me: God did not come to rescue us from this planet; God became it. When I grieve the planet, I am grieving the very body of God.

A CALL TO HOLY ANGER

The systems of power want us to be paralyzed by our grief. They want us to feel small, overwhelmed, and hopeless, so that we do nothing. They want to individualize the crisis, making us obsess over our personal carbon footprint while they continue to burn the world for profit.

But our grief is not just sorrow. It is a holy, righteous anger. It is the Image of God in us screaming, "This is wrong."

This anger is anything but sin; it is a sacred fuel. It is your love for this world refusing to be silent. We are not called to be nice in the face of this catastrophe. We are not called to be polite. We are called to be faithful. And faithfulness, right now, looks a lot like defiance.

ENCOURAGEMENT FOR YOUR DAY

This is the non-negotiable faith we are called to. We must have the courage to hold both truths at once: We can grieve the melting ice, and we can plant the tree.

We can mourn what is lost, and we can fight like hell for what is left.

This is the only hope that matters. Hope is not a passive feeling we wait for; it is a discipline. It is a defiant choice to act as if a better world is possible, and to build it with our own two hands.

So do the act. Make the call. Join the protest. Divest your money. Change your consumption. Have the hard, impolite conversation at the dinner table. Your small, faithful no to the systems of death, and your small, defiant yes to life, is the very practice of Advent.

A BLESSING FOR TODAY

O Holy One, Creator of soil, skin, and breath: Forgive us our complicity and our silence. Do not grant us a cheap "peace" that makes us comfortable with injustice. Grant us the holy fire of your love for this world. Radicalize our hearts. Make our grief a shovel. Make our anger a seed. Make our love a revolution. Amen.

December 15

Ancestors at the Manger

We are people who crave connection. We long for roots, for a story that holds us. Yet, the image of Christmas we have been handed is often a profound source of disconnection. It is a clean, quiet, sentimental, and overwhelmingly white European story. Not surprisingly many people balk at this image, sensing in their bones that it's not honest.

But the story in Matthew is far messier, browner, and more complicated. It is a story of colonized people, of refugees, and of a very complex family tree. When we look closer, we find that the manger is not an isolated, sterile scene.

UNPACKING THE SCRIPTURE

We are trained to skip the "begats"—the long genealogy in Matthew 1 that opens the Gospel. Our eyes glaze over. We see it as a boring list of patriarchal names. In doing so, we miss the first, radical deconstruction in the New Testament.

Matthew, a Jewish writer for a Jewish audience, does something subversive. He shatters the traditional patriarchal lineage by intentionally including the names of five women. And look at who he names:

- **Tamar:** A woman who survived injustice by tricking her own father-in-law in a scandalous act of self-preservation. (Read Genesis 38 for the full story, but be warned, it's worse than you think)
- **Rahab:** A non-Israelite, a foreigner, and a sex worker, who became a crucial link through her own act of defiance.
- **Ruth:** A refugee from a rival nation, a woman defined by poverty, loyalty, and her outsider status.
- **Bathsheba:** A woman whose name is carried in a story of power, sexual assault, murder, and profound trauma.
- **Mary:** A young, unwed woman in a high-risk, scandalous pregnancy.

This is not a list of the pure, the perfect, or the proper. This is a list of survivors, foreigners, the traumatized, and the marginalized. Matthew is making a stunning theological claim, right at the top: God's story is not built on perfect bloodlines, but on resilient ones. God chooses the messy, the complicated, the excluded, and the unworthy to birth the Holy.

THE LIVED REALITY

As a pastor, I have sat with so many people in pastoral care visits, in hospital rooms, and in funeral conversations, who carry a deep, quiet psychological shame about their messy family stories. I have seen the universal human impulse to create a clean, respectable identity, to hide the parts of the family story that don't fit a perfect image.

I have learned, from listening to them, that this shame is a profound wound. It cuts people off from their roots and from the very ground of their being.

What Matthew's genealogy teaches me, and what I try to bring to that holy, pastoral space, is that God does not wait for us to be pure to show up. God is in the mess.

The resilience of Tamar, the defiance of Rahab, the loyalty of Ruth, the survival of Bathsheba—these are not barriers to the holy. They are the path. I have come to see that when we disown our ancestors' messy stories, we disown the very places God has already been at work.

An Encouragement for Your Day

The invitation for today is to look at your own story with new eyes.

If your family is a source of pain or disconnection... if your heritage is complicated... if you are decolonizing your faith and feel adrift... the Gospel says to you: **"Your story belongs."**

Your ancestors, with all their resilience, all their flaws, and all their deep, unhealed wounds, are not a source of shame. They are a testament to survival. Their complicated lives are the very soil from which you have grown. You are the fruit of their profound, and often painful, "yes" to life.

A Blessing for Today

O Holy One, God of our ancestors, God of Tamar, and Rahab, and Ruth, and Bathsheba. We thank you for the survivors. We thank you for the complicated, messy, and resilient ones who endured so that we might be here. This Advent, heal our shame. Help us to honour our own stories, not as a problem to be fixed, but as the sacred, fertile, and holy ground where you are, right now, being born in us. Amen.

December 16

Rewriting the Naughty/Nice List

Let's be honest: this is the high season of the great, cosmic scorekeeping. I'll confess, I still feel the anxiety of the Naughty or Nice list. It's that invisible, spiritual ledger where I feel I'm being tallied. Did I do enough? Was I good enough? This isn't just a children's story; it's the default spirituality I've internalized. It's the belief that my worth is a performance review. It is, frankly, exhausting.

So, let's propose a holy rebellion. Let's retire naughty or nice. Let's try this instead: Did I repair harm? And did I receive grace?

UNPACKING THE SCRIPTURE

The Apostle Paul, a man who was the absolute gold standard of religious perfectionism—a "Naughty/Nice" list expert—had to have his entire system broken apart to understand grace. He's a "recovering perfectionist." And he writes this:

> "For by grace you have been saved through faith, and this is not your own doing; it is the gift of God —not the result of works, so that no one may boast." (Ephesians 2:8-9)

This is the great dismantling of all scorekeeping. Paul is describing a shift from the transactional world ("I do this, God gives me that") to the relational world ("I am held, therefore I am free"). The manger is not a reward for a nice world. It is a gift to a messy, complicated, "naughty," and completely undeserving world.

THE LIVED REALITY

I've had to learn that, psychologically, my brain loves a ledger. That Naughty/Nice list isn't just a story for kids; it's the default operating system for the anxious, scorekeeping part of my mind. It's the part that needs this binary system to know its own worth, which it can only ever measure through comparison and being right.

I know from my own life that this is a spiritual dead-end. It guarantees anxiety because that inner scorekeeper can never be perfect enough to satisfy itself.

The spiritual path I'm learning to walk operates in an entirely different economy. It doesn't live by the ledger; it lives by grace. It's the part of me that is slowly learning my worth is not a performance but a given. It is not earned; it is received.

This is the crucial distinction: Santa's list is about earning. The manger is about receiving.

Now, grace doesn't mean no consequences—I've learned that's just my inner scorekeeper trying to find a loophole. It just means my worth is not on the line. Grace replaces the childish binary of Naughty/Nice with the grown-up, human work of repair.

My inner scorekeeper asks, Am I good or am I bad?. My healing, human heart asks, Is there harm? How do I mend?

ENCOURAGEMENT FOR YOUR DAY

The invitation for today is to tear up the list. Stop the scorekeeping, just for today. When you mess up (and you will, because you are human), refuse to go down the "I am a naughty/bad person" rabbit hole. That's just the inner scorekeeper indulging in self-obsession.

Instead, practice the two questions of a grace-filled, adult faith:

1. "Did I cause harm?" If the answer is yes, the follow-up isn't, "Am I terrible?" It's, "How do I repair it?"

2. "Did I receive grace?" When I failed, did I allow myself to be loved anyway? When someone else failed, did I offer them compassion instead of adding a mark to their ledger?

A BLESSING FOR TODAY

O Holy One, Giver of all good gifts: Save us from the tyranny of the ledger. Release us from the frantic, exhausting need to earn our own worth. Quiet the inner scorekeeper that tells us we are not enough. When we cause harm, grant us the holy courage to repair. And when we are offered love, grant us the profound humility to simply... receive. May our Advent be defined not by our perfection, but by your presence. Amen.

DECEMBER 17

You Are Not Too Much, and You Are Not Too Late

There is a profound, quiet shame many of us carry. It is the secret, haunting belief that we are, in some fundamental way, wrong.

I know this voice. It is the voice of too much; you are too loud, too emotional, too sensitive, too neurodivergent, too queer, too skeptical. Your very being feels like a problem for a world that demands conformity.

And it is the voice of too late: you are behind. You haven't healed, you haven't arrived. Advent can feel like a judgment on those of us who are not ready.

But the Advent story itself is the antidote to this shame.

UNPACKING THE SCRIPTURE

We must deconstruct the clean, perfect pageant we've created: the one we see in nativity scenes. It only takes a careful reading of Matthew and Luke to learn that this scene, with shepherds and Magi kneeling together, doesn't exist in the Bible. It's a mash-up of two separate stories, in two different Gospels, telling two different truths to two different audiences from two different world views. I've found that when we pull them apart, their power gets stronger.

First, in Luke's Gospel, God invites the shepherds. Let's be clear: these are the unclean, messy, marginalized gig-economy workers of their day. They are the too much. And God bypasses the clean, the religious, and the "ready" to invite them first.

Then, in Matthew's Gospel, we get the Magi. These are the "too late". They are the too skeptical, the weirdo mystics, the astrologers from the wrong religion. They miss the birth entirely. By the time they arrive, Jesus is a toddler. And what happens? They are not turned away. Their late arrival is still held up as an Epiphany, a revelation of God.

When we read them this way, the truth is clear: Both Gospels independently tell a story that dismantles our ideas of purity and punctuality.

THE LIVED REALITY

I have had to learn that the "too much" and "too late" voice is the internalized voice of a culture that demands conformity. It's the part of my mind that lives by comparison. It's the inner critic that has learned to measure my worth against an imaginary "normal" standard, a standard that is most often white, male, euro-centric, straight, and neurotypical.

I've learned that this inner critic is the part of me that believes the lie that my worth is conditional on my performance or my timeliness.

The spiritual path I'm learning is that grace is not about God overlooking my lateness or my "too much-ness." Grace is the revelation that God does not even use those measurements. The manger is the place where the culture's metrics (productivity, normalcy, timeliness) are rendered utterly irrelevant.

Encouragement for Your Day

The invitation for today is to stop believing the voice of cultural comparison.

Your "too much-ness": your sensitivity, your passion, your queerness, your doubt, is not a barrier to the Holy. It is the very location where the Holy is waiting to meet you.

Your "lateness": your messy, unfinished, not-ready life, is not a failure. It is simply the time and place of your actual life. And that is the exact time and place God ever shows up.

You are not late. You are not too much. You are, in fact, right on time, and you are exactly the person God is looking for.

A Blessing for Today

O Holy One, God of the messy and the late, God of the shepherds and the Magi: Quiet the inner voice of shame that tells us we are 'too much' or 'too far behind.' Let us see our lives not as a problem to be solved, but as a story to be held. May we arrive at the manger, exactly as we are— sensitive, struggling, late, and beloved— and may we, at last, find ourselves welcomed and at home. Amen.

DECEMBER 18

The Divine Isn't Far Off, It's Right Here

Let us be honest. For many of us, the "God" we were handed is a problem. It is the image of a distant, angry judge; a cosmic scorekeeper; a "Sky God" who is separate from the world, watching us with disappointment.

And let us be even more honest: this God has been used to justify violence, to enforce shame, and to legitimize systems of oppression. If this is the God you have walked away from, the God you are deconstructing, the God you can no longer believe in... you are not faithless. You are, perhaps, just finally waking up.

Because what if that God is not the God of Advent? What if the Divine is not far off at all? What if, as the mystics have always taught, God is in the breath, the skin, the soil—right here?

UNPACKING THE SCRIPTURE

The central, explosive claim of this season is the Incarnation. But to understand it, I've had to unlearn some lessons I was first heard in Sunday School.

I was told the good news was an escape plan. It was about a distant "Sky God" who was angry at the world, and a Jesus who came to help us escape that world and get up there to that God.

But this is not the Gospel Jesus preached. When Jesus began his work, his very first words were a deconstruction of that distant God:

> "Repent, for the kingdom of heaven has come near." (Matthew 4:17b)

I've had to learn that repent (*metanoia* in the greek) doesn't mean feel bad. It means change your perception or see in a new way. And what are we to see? That the kingdom is not up there. It has come near. It is at hand. It is here.

This is the ultimate anti-"Sky God" message. Jesus's entire ministry was not about an escape from this world. It was a revelation about this world: the Divine is not distant and separate; rather the Divine is immediately available, right here, right now, in the flesh.

THE LIVED REALITY

This opened my eyes to see that the the cosmic scorekeeper, the angry judge, was a projection. It was the part of our culture (and my mind) that needed a dualistic world of "up/down," "in/out," "judge/judged". It was a God of control, an idea my conditioned mind used to feel superior or to manage its fear.

The spiritual path I'm learning to walk is one that doesn't need this separation. It's the path of the mystics, the internal but ancient wisdom that knows, on a pre-rational level, that I am not separate from God.

It's the wisdom that God isn't a distant object to be believed in, but the Ground of all Being; the very life that lives in and through all things.

When I deconstruct the "Sky God," I'm not losing my faith. I'm shedding the mind's projection to make space for a real encounter.

This, for me, is the true, radical meaning of Incarnation. It is not a story about God visiting the world. It is the revelation that God *is* the world —that the Divine is not separate, but is the very lifeblood within our world.

Encouragement for Your Day

The invitation for today is to stop searching for a distant God out there and to practice noticing the God who is right here.

This is the meaning of a mystical, incarnational faith. You do not have to go to a special building or achieve a special state of purity to find the Holy.

The sacred is in your next, ordinary breath. (God is the air). The sacred is in the soil under your feet. (God is the ground). The sacred is in the face of your neighbour. (God is the other). And, most radically, the sacred is in your own skin. (God is your own life).

If you have left organized religion, you are not an exile from the Divine. You are, perhaps, just a mystic in training, finally searching for the real thing.

A Blessing for Today

O Holy One, Ground of all Being, You who are as close as our own skin, as near as our own breath: Forgive us for looking "up there" for what has always been "right here." Heal us from the lie that you are separate from us. This Advent, may we stop searching for a distant God, and simply open our hearts to the Divine Life that is breathing us, holding us, and living as us, right now, in this very moment. Amen.

DECEMBER 19

Chosen Family at the Manger

This season, the word "family" is used as both a balm and a weapon. It is in every song, every advertisement. For those whose biological family is a source of safety and love, this is a season of simple joy. And, for many, that word is also a source of profound grief.

And so we must be ruthlessly honest about the whole story we are telling. Because the story we've been sold: the pristine, traditional family on the Christmas card, isn't the only story. It is not the whole story of the Gospel.

The first Christmas was a chosen family story.

UNPACKING THE SCRIPTURE

We must deconstruct the sentimental, respectable pageant we have created. The cast of characters at the first nativity is a collection of outsiders, a band of un-respectables brought together by a Divine call. Look at them:

- **Mary:** A young, unwed, pregnant teenager in a situation of profound scandal and danger.

- **Joseph:** Her confused fiancé, who is not the biological father. He has to make a choice. He must actively choose to stay, to protect, and to form this family, against all cultural and religious purity codes.

- **The Shepherds:** Not considered polite company. They were the unclean, messy, unreliable strangers from the fields, the last people you would invite into your home.

This is not a traditional family. This is a found family, this is a chosen family. This is a queer little band of outsiders and refugees, held together not by bloodline or social approval, but by a radical, chosen yes. This story queers the very definition of family, tearing it away from blood and soil and re-grounding it in chosen love and mutual care.

THE LIVED REALITY

I want to be honest here: this theme is not just theological for me. It is, I've come to realize, the central message in everything I write. I have an amazing, supportive blood family, so let's be clear: this is not a rejection of blood family.

But I know, both as a pastor and as a human, that the psychological grief of rejection is a real death. We are wired for belonging. And when we begin the brave, human work of deconstruction, or when we heal from religious harm, that path can be lonely. It can, and often does, put us at odds with the very people and forms that were supposed to be our home.

The agony of that non-belonging is the dark night that forces us to ask a new question. We are forced to stop clinging to the form of family and instead search for the content of love.

This is the path I am on. I've recently had the magical and divine experience of finding a new community, my people, who value me for exactly who I am. And this is the truth I have learned: the family you make: the friends who become siblings, the community that chooses you, is not second best. It is the profound, human revelation of the Gospel. It is that magical and divine feeling of being seen, and it is the living, breathing, here-and-now presence of God.

Encouragement for Your Day

The invitation for today is to honour the holiness of your found family.

Your worth is not, and has never been, dependent on your family of origin. The incarnation itself proves that God is always found with the excluded, in the non-traditional, among the chosen.

The family that chooses you, that celebrates you, that fights for you... that is the Holy family. Your love for them, and their love for you, is not a consolation prize. It is the living, breathing, incarnate presence of God.

A Blessing for Today

O Holy One, God of the chosen and the found, God of the friend who is closer than a sibling: My heart is so full of gratitude for the love that chooses me, for the community that holds me. And that very joy creates in me a deep ache for anyone who does not feel that same abundance. For all who are grieving the family they were born into, for all who feel the sting of a complicated family, for all who are lonely—pour out a healing balm. And bless, with a fierce and holy light, the sacred, chosen families we have made. May our love for one another be our Advent defiance, a testament to a God who builds a home for all who have been left outside. Amen.

December 20

No Room at the Inn: Housing Is a Sacred Right

As a pastor in this community, I find it harder each year to reconcile the festive spirit of the season with the harsh reality I see every day. I see our neighbours, our fellow citizens, without secure housing. I see a critical lack of services for those in dire need.

We are lighting candles and preparing for carols, all while the 'inns' of our own community are full.

We must be brutally honest. We have turned a story of systemic failure into a cozy pageant, and it is time to stop.

If the Holy was nearly born on the street, housing justice is Advent work.

UNPACKING THE SCRIPTURE

The single, devastating line that pivots the entire Advent story is this:

> "...because there was no room for them in the inn."
> (Luke 2:7b)

We have sentimentalized this, imagining a flustered but kind innkeeper. I have come to see the text as colder and more systemic. It is a statement of exclusion. The inn, the place of community and safety, had no space for a poor, displaced, colonized family on the margins.

Here's the truth I hold onto: this is not a quiet story. It is a story of a housing crisis. It is a story of a refugee crisis (the flight to Egypt). It is a story of state-sanctioned violence (Herod's massacre). God does not incarnate into a silent night; God shows up directly in the heart of political oppression, economic displacement, and a total failure of social hospitality.

THE LIVED REALITY

Harsh truth: The sentimental pageant is a powerful defense mechanism. It allows us to feel spiritual and festive while participating in a system that leaves creates people out in the cold with no room.

It is the profound, human psychological split that allows us to sing 'O Holy Night' on Sunday and vote against affordable housing on Monday night without ever feeling the contradiction.

When we let ourselves feel that contradiction, the natural human response is rage.

This is a holy anger. It is not a bad. It is not a failure of faith. It is the image of God in us screaming that this "holy night" cannot be "silent" when our neighbours are in crisis. This anger is a gift. It is the sacred fuel we need to actually do the work.

This is the truth of the Gospel: we cannot praise the God who was born in a barn and simultaneously criminalize our neighbours for sleeping in one. This is not a political opinion; it is the central, non-negotiable claim of the story.

ENCOURAGEMENT FOR YOUR DAY

The invitation of Advent is not to feel festive. The invitation is to make room. To be clear, "making room" is not a metaphor, it is a job.

It is the hard, holy, hand-on work of building.

Where is the Holy Family in our town tonight? They are in the shelter. They are in the tent encampment. They are on the social housing waiting list.

Our Advent work, then, is clear. It is the personal work of supporting that shelter, donating, bringing a meal. And it is the systemic work of showing up at city council, of writing to our representatives, of demanding that our "inn" be a place of justice, not just of commerce.

A BLESSING FOR TODAY

O Holy One, You who were born with "no room," You who are still found among those with no safe place to sleep: Forgive us. Forgive us for our comfortable inns. Forg-ive us for our sentimentality that costs us nothing and changes nothing. Break our hearts with the truth of your story, and then make our hands the tools of your justice. This Advent, may we stop singing about the manger and start building one. Amen.

DECEMBER 21

The Longest Night: Grief and Empty Chairs

Today is the longest night of the year. Here in the Northern Hemisphere where I am writing, the darkness is at its deepest.

And for many of us, the festive season mirrors this darkness. We are told to be merry, but our hearts are heavy. There is an empty chair at the table, a name we ache to say, a future that is not what we planned.

Today, we will not perform. We will not fix it. We will not look on the bright side.

Today, we will simply be honest. We will honour the holy, human, and necessary work of grief. This, too, is Advent.

A CRY IN THE DARK

The language for this dark night is not found in a carol, but in the raw honesty of the Psalms:

> "My God, my God, why have you forsaken me? Why are you so far from helping me, from the words of my groaning? O my God, I cry by day, but you do not answer; and by night, but find no rest." (Psalm 22:1-2)

This is the most honest prayer in the world. It is the cry of a heart that is not pretending. At it's best, our faith tradition does not demand our silence; it gives us a language for our pain. This is the *sound* of faith in a real, honest and meaningful relationship with God. It is the prayer Jesus himself cried from the cross. It is an ache that demands to be spoken. Today, we don't run from this cry. We join it. We honour it. We make space for it.

A LITANY OF HOLY REMEMBRANCE

Today, we light a candle against the dark and name the truth of what we carry.

We remember the grief that is fresh and raw, and the grief that is old, returning with the season.

We remember the empty chair at the table and the silence where a voice we loved should be.

We remember the loss of a partner, a parent, a child—a grief that rewrites the world.

We remember the loss of a friend, a sibling, a chosen-family member.

We remember the love of a pet, a companion whose non-human life held our whole heart, a love that is real, profound, and often dismissed.

We remember the loss of a dream, a job, or a future we were counting on.

We remember the grief of a faith we have had to leave behind.

We do not grieve in spite of our love. We grieve because of it. Our grief is not an obstacle to the holy; it is the measure of our love.

A Promise in the Dark

This is the hard, beautiful paradox of our faith: that same tradition that holds the raw cry of Psalm 22 also holds this defiant, unshakeable promise:

> "For I am convinced that neither death, nor life, nor angels, nor rulers, nor things present, nor things to come, nor powers, nor height, nor depth, nor anything else in all creation, will be able to separate us from the love of God in Christ Jesus our Lord." (Romans 8:38-39)

I want to be clear: this is not a platitude. This is not a silver lining that erases the pain of Psalm 22. This is a fierce and deeply human promise, written by a man who knew suffering.

It is a promise of presence. It does not try to say we will not feel separated; our grief is real, and it feels like a canyon. It says that in reality, nothing, not even the finality of death, has the power to sever the cord of love that binds us to the Holy and to one another. God is not on the other side of our grief. God is in it with us.

A Blessing For the Longest Night

This is not an encouragement. It is not an invitation to do anything at all. It is a blessing. So, just for this moment, I invite you to stop. To breathe. To lay down the burden of being festive. You do not have to perform.

May you be gentle with yourself.

May you have the holy courage to not be "okay."

May you have the clarity to recognize your grief and the strength to name it, without trying to avoid its holy, human weight.

May you have the vulnerability to let your people show up, to allow those close to you to offer help, to sit with you, and to care for you when you need it.

May you treat your own sorrow with the same reverence you would offer a sacred text, for it is that holy.

May you find a quiet corner to simply sit in the truth of your own heart, without apology.

May you, in this deepest dark, feel the quiet, unshakeable presence of a God who is not afraid of your grief.

May you know, in your bones, that the Holy One is not on the other side of your pain, but in it with you, holding the broken shards of your heart alongside you.

And may you trust that this, too, is Advent: this holy, honest, silent waiting in the dark. Amen.

DECEMBER 22

Justice Is the Gospel

For most of our lives, the gospel has been presented as a personal salvation plan. We were told the Good News was a transaction—a get out of hell free card for our individual souls. It was a spirituality of escape: if we believed the right things, we would be rescued from this broken, messy world and taken to a heaven somewhere else.

I must be honest: this was my preferred gospel for the first two decades of my life. It's the one I was taught. It's individualistic, transactional, and easier. It required no real, costly change to my life or my complicity in the systems around me.

But this is not the gospel of advent. Heaven isn't an escape—it's justice breaking in."

UNPACKING THE SCRIPTURE

We must ask: What was the original good news? It was not some theological formula, it was a song, sung by a young, poor, colonized woman. The Magnificat is the first, and perhaps most crystal clear description of the Gospel.

When Mary learns what God is doing, what does she proclaim this good news is?

> "He has brought down the powerful from their thrones, and lifted up the lowly; He has filled the hungry with good things, and sent the rich away empty." (Luke 1:52-53)

This is the Gospel. It is not a maybe someday spiritual promise. It is the good news to the poor that the systems crushing them are being dismantled. It is the good news to the hungry that they will be fed. And it is the hard, prophetic news to the powerful that their time is up.

THE LIVED REALITY

The personal escape gospel is a powerful defense mechanism. It gives us room us to separate our faith (a private, spiritual feeling) from our lives (our politics, our economics, our complicity in systems of harm).

I know this impulse. It's the part of me that wants to feel saved while still hoarding, still climbing, still participating in the very systems of Empire that Jesus confronted. It's a faith that costs me nothing.

But the path I am learning to walk is one that knows God is not out there. It knows God is in this with us: in the mud, in the flesh. Therefore, the Advent gospel cannot be about escaping the world; it must be about healing the world.

This, for me, is the great truth of our faith: Heaven isn't an escape plan; it's a renovation project.

The Gospel is the announcement that God's kingdom of justice and wholeness is not a future destination, but a present-tense reality that is breaking in, right here, right now, demanding our participation.

ENCOURAGEMENT FOR YOUR DAY

The invitation for today is to stop waiting to be rescued and to start participating in the renovation.

Your faith is not about securing your ticket out. Your faith is about receiving your assignment here.

Where are the thrones of power that need dismantling? Where are the hungry who need to be filled? The good news isn't just something you believe; it's something you get involved in. It is the hard, holy, hands-dirty work of getting in the way of injustice and building shalom with the very life God has given you.

A BLESSING FOR TODAY

O Holy One, God of the Revolution, God of Mary: Forgive us for making your "Good News" so small, so tame, and so selfish. Forgive us for making it about 'me' instead of 'us.' Burn Mary's song into our hearts, and put the tools of your great renovation project into our hands. This Advent, may we not just wait for your kingdom, but build it. Amen.

December 23

A Blessing for Tired Caregivers

This, today, is not for everyone. This is for a specific, holy, and exhausted group of people.

This is for the ones who are carrying other people's needs in your heart. This is for the caregivers.

It is December 23rd, and the world is demanding "magic." But you are the one who knows the magic is, in fact, just labour. It is *your* labour.

You are the one making the lists, buying the groceries, setting up the decorations, wrapping the gifts. You are the one who will clean up. You are the one managing everyone else's emotions, holding the grief for those who are gone, and absorbing the meltdowns of those who are present. You are the nurse, the therapist, the parent, the child caring for an aging parent.

And here is the deep, aching irony: You are the one creating the magic, but you are too tired to feel it. You are so busy making sure everyone else is okay that no one has stopped to ask if *you* are.

To the Saints carrying the Manger,

I'm writing this letter to you.

I see you. And I want to use that word **Saints** because in my tradition, saints were never perfect, magical people. They were real humans, flawes and beautiful. They were the people whose hands-on, human work was so shot-through with love that it became the very work of God.

And that is what I see you doing.

I know that the original nativity story was not a Hallmark "Silent Night." It was labour. It was the story of a young, exhausted, terrified woman, doing the single most profound, "in-the-flesh" work a human can do. It was blood, and fear, and sweat, and fatigue.

The Holy One did not just appear. The Holy One had to be birthed, through the messy, agonizing, sacred, physical work of a caregiver.

Your story, your exhaustion, is not a distraction from the Christmas story. It *is* the Christmas story.

I know the psychological lie that can drive you. It's the voice that says your worth is earned by your service. "If I create a perfect Christmas, if I meet everyone's needs, then I am a good person." I know that voice. It is the path to burnout, resentment, and a profound, hollow loneliness.

But the spiritual path I am learning is that our worth is not in our doing, but in our being.

Your profound, bone-deep fatigue is not a sign that you are failing at Christmas. Your fatigue is the sacred, physical evidence of your love. It is your *kenosis:* your holy self-emptying. The invisible, thankless, endless work you do: that is not magic. That is the in-the-flesh work of God.

So just for a moment... and let these words be for you.

For the one who has been carrying everyone else's hearts.... For the one who is the quiet, exhausted engine of everyone else's joy... For the one whose love has become an invisible, endless, aching labour...

May you, for one moment, set it down. May you feel your own worth, separate from what you do for anyone else. May a moment of quiet, unburdened peace find you. May you, just once, be shown the same profound, gentle, and unconditional care that you so freely give. May you know, in your bones, that you are not just the caregiver.

You are the beloved.

You are seen.

You are loved.

Amen.

December 24

Joy Is a Form of Resistance

It is Christmas Eve. And there is a profound guilt that many of us carry into this night. We look at the world, which is aching. We see the injustice, the poverty, the climate crisis, our own grief. And in the face of all that suffering, our own joy feels perhaps frivolous. Disrespectful. A betrayal, even.

But this is the most effective lie that the systems of death and despair have ever told.

We must reclaim the most dangerous, subversive, and holy act of this season. Joy doesn't ignore injustice—it sings in its face.

Unpacking the Scripture

The first, explosive announcement of the Gospel was not a complicated theological treatise. It was a song, interrupting the darkest night for the most marginalized people.

> "Do not be afraid; for see—I am bringing you good news of great joy for all the people!" (Luke 2:10)

This is the key. The angel does not say, "I am bringing you good news once you have fixed the world." The angel does not say, "Here is a feeling of joy because your Roman occupation is over."

No. The joy is the interruption. The joy is the announcement. The joy is given in the midst of the occupation, in the midst of the darkness, to the poor.

This is not "toxic positivity," which pretends the darkness isn't real. This is subversive joy, which looks the darkness right in the eye and announces that it does not get the final word.

THE LIVED REALITY

I've learned that my joy guilt comes from a conditioned, binary part of my mind. It's the part without spectrums, that believes we can only choose one thing: happy *or* sad.

But we all know intrinsically that we can be many things at the same time. It's the deep, human wisdom that has the capacity to hold the world's suffering and our personal grief in one hand, and at the same time hold the unshakeable, foundational joy of God's presence in the other.

This is the wisdom our womanist and liberationist ancestors knew in their bones. The joy that sang spirituals in the face of slavery was not frivolous. It was the fuel that kept them going in unspeakably awful times.

Oppressive systems need us to be burnt out, hopeless, and joyless. Because joyless people are so much easier to control. Subversive joy is the sustenance for the long, hard work of justice. It is the holy "no" to despair.

ENCOURAGEMENT FOR YOUR DAY

The invitation for tonight, on this holy, dark, and joyful night, is to commit a small act of holy resistance.

Your laughter tonight is not a betrayal of faith; it is your faith in action. Your song is a "no" in the face of complacent silence. The food you share is not an indulgence; it is a testament that creation is good and worth fighting for.

Do not feel guilty for your joy. Your joy is your fuel. It is your right. It is your holy, defiant act of telling the darkness that it has not won, and it never will.

A BLESSING FOR TODAY

O Holy One, God of Subversive Joy, You who brought a song in the middle of the night: Grant us the audacity to be joyful tonight. Grant us the courage to laugh, to sing, and to feast. In a world that profits from our despair, make our joy our most profound and holy act of resistance. May it be the fuel that heals us, and the fire that lights the world. Amen.

A blessed, defiant, and truly Merry Christmas to you.

December 25

Awakening to God's Nearness

Merry Christmas.

First, before anything else, I want to say thank you. Thank you for walking this Advent path with me. This journey, for us, has not been about a clean, sentimental countdown. We have, I hope, been honest. We've sat with the ache of perfectionism, the holy rage at injustice, the grief of a planet in crisis, and the deep, sacred questions about our faith. We've talked about our beautifully odd brains, our complicated families, and our holy defiance.

We've refused to settle for a cheap, easy holiday. And now, after all that honest, messy, and real waiting, we are here.

So what is the point?

After all the noise, the paper, the food, and the frantic pressure to feel a certain way, what is the one, single, revolutionary idea at the bottom of it all?

Here it is:

Love became flesh and blood and moved into our neighbourhood... and it is still doing so.

The great, earth-shattering story of Christmas is not simply that a thing happened then; that a baby was born in a specific, historical moment.

The point is that it is happening now.

FINAL BLESSING

My friends, thank you for sharing this journey. Thank you for being willing to sit in the messy, honest, and holy questions.

My blessing for you on this Christmas Day is simple, and it is the truest thing I know:

Merry Christmas. You are the beloved of God. You are, right now, in this very breath, shot through with the Divine.

Go live like it.

With all my gratitude and peace,

Greg

www.ingramcontent.com/pod-product-compliance
Lightning Source LLC
Chambersburg PA
CBHW071218070526
44584CB00019B/3071